Journey of a Book

John Malam

www.raintreepublishers.co.uk
Visit our website to find out
more information about
Raintree books.

To order:
☏ Phone 0845 6044371
🖷 Fax +44 (0) 1865 312263
📧 Email myorders@raintreepublishers.co.uk

Customers from outside the UK please telephone +44 1865 312262

Raintree is an imprint of Capstone Global Library Limited,
a company incorporated in England and Wales having its
registered office at 7 Pilgrim Street, London, EC4V 6LB –
Registered company number: 6695582

Text © Capstone Global Library Limited 2012

First published in hardback in 2012

Edited by Dan Nunn and Diyan Leake
Designed by Cynthia Della-Rovere
Original illustrations © Capstone Global Library Ltd 2012
Illustrated by Capstone Global Library Ltd
Picture research by Mica Brancic
Production by Alison Parsons
Originated by Capstone Global Library Ltd
Printed and bound in China by Leo Paper Products Ltd

ISBN 978 1 406 23932 4 (hardback)
16 15 14 13 12
10 9 8 7 6 5 4 3 2 1

British Library Cataloguing in Publication Data
Malam, John, 1957–

Journey of a book.

002-dc22

A full catalogue record for this book is available from the
British Library.

Acknowledgements
The author and publishers are grateful to the following for
permission to reproduce copyright material: © Capstone
Global Library Ltd (Lord and Leverett) pp. 1, 3, 4, 9,
10, 11, 12, 14, 15, 17, 18, 19, 29 top, 31; © Capstone
Publishers (Karon Dubke) p. 16; Corbis pp. 5 (Blend
Images/© Shannon Fagan), 28 (Zefa/© Matthias Tunger),
29 bottom (Blend Images/© Shannon Fagan); Doug
Parsons p. 27; Getty Images (Radius Images) p. 6; © Leo
Paper Products pp. 21, 22, 23, 24, 25; Shutterstock pp. 7
(© Goodluz), 26 (© J. van der Wolf).

Cover photograph of a pile of books and photograph of a
library of books reproduced with permission of © Capstone
Global Library Ltd (Lord & Leverett); photograph of a
notebook for notes with horizontal stripes reproduced wth
permission of Shutterstock (© Matti).

Every effort has been made to contact copyright holders
of material reproduced in this book. Any omissions will be
rectified in subsequent printings if notice is given to the
publisher.

Contents

Some words are shown in bold, **like this**. You can find out what they mean by looking in the Glossary.

What will you read?

It's good to read a book! It could be a comic book, a poetry book, a joke book, a pop-up book, or a **fiction** book. The book in your hands right now is a **non-fiction** book.

There are so many books to choose from!

I wonder how my book was made.

Have you ever wondered how a book is made? Where do the ideas come from? How do the pictures get on to the pages? A book has an interesting journey on its way to your bookshelves, as you are about to find out.

It's all about teamwork

It takes a lot of people to make a book. They work together as a team. Each person in the team does a different job. Little by little, the book comes together.

Everyone in the team does a different job.

These are some of the people in the team that make a book: **author**, **editor**, **illustrator**, **picture researcher**, **photographer**, and **designer**. You will find out about them in this book.

Good ideas

A book starts with someone having a good idea. If it is a **fiction** book, the idea usually comes from an **author**. The author sends the idea to a **publishing company**. If the company likes the author's idea, it might turn it into a book.

This author is going to post her fiction book idea.

The editor describes a non-fiction book idea.

If it is a **non-fiction** book, it is usually an **editor** who has the idea for it. The editor works for the publishing company. They ask an author to write the book.

Author and editor

The editor talks to the author about the book.

Authors work with **editors**. For a **fiction** book, the author and editor will talk about the story. The editor might make suggestions. This could be very helpful for the author. For a **non-fiction** book, the editor tells the author what the book should be like.

The editor of this book told the author that the book should have 32 pages. He said there should be two to four sentences on each page. He also said what age the book should be for (your age), and whether it should have photographs or **illustrations**.

This author is talking to her editor about her book.

Right!
Where's Eddie?

Hide and Seek

Writing a plan

The **author** writes a plan, or outline, for the book. This sets out what will be in the book, from beginning to end. It helps the author to write the book. It also tells the **editor** what the author is going to write about.

A plan can be a list of ideas.

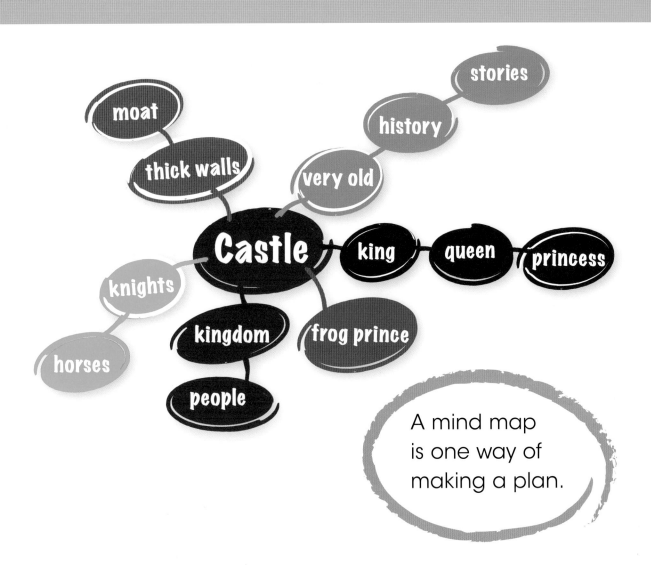

A mind map is one way of making a plan.

Fiction authors have a good **imagination**. Their plan shows the ideas they have for their story. **Non-fiction** authors are good at finding information. Their plan shows the facts they will write about.

Writing the book

The **author** writes the book, following the plan as closely as possible. Most authors type their books straight on to a computer. Some authors write their books on paper, then type them up.

This author is writing her book.

The editor is the first person to read the book.

When the author finishes writing the book, he or she sends it to another **editor**. The editor reads it very carefully. Sometimes the editor asks the author to make changes, or to double-check facts.

Photographs and illustrations

A **non-fiction** book usually has photographs in it. A person called a **picture researcher** finds the photographs. The picture researcher might borrow the photographs from a picture library. A **photographer** might take some of the photographs.

A photographer may work in a studio.

This illustrator is adding colour to an illustration.

Fiction books often have **illustrations**. Some non-fiction books do, too. **Illustrators** first do their drawings in pencil. Then they colour them in with felt-tip pens, pencil crayons, or paints. Some illustrators use computers to make their pictures.

Setting out the pages

Every book needs a **designer**. Designers decide where to set out the words, photographs, and **illustrations** of a book. They also choose which **font** to use for the letters, and what colours to use for backgrounds.

This designer is using a scanner to get an illustration on to a computer.

computer

scanner

The designer is working out where to put the words and pictures on a page.

Where is Eddie?
Is he **on** the cat or **under** the cat?

9

Designers set out books on a computer, page by page. They move the words and pictures around on the computer screen until they are in the best place. They make sure everything looks good.

To the printer

After the **designer** has set the book out, it is ready for printing. Books are printed in **factories** all over the world. This book was printed in China. You can see the name of the **printing company** on the second page of this book.

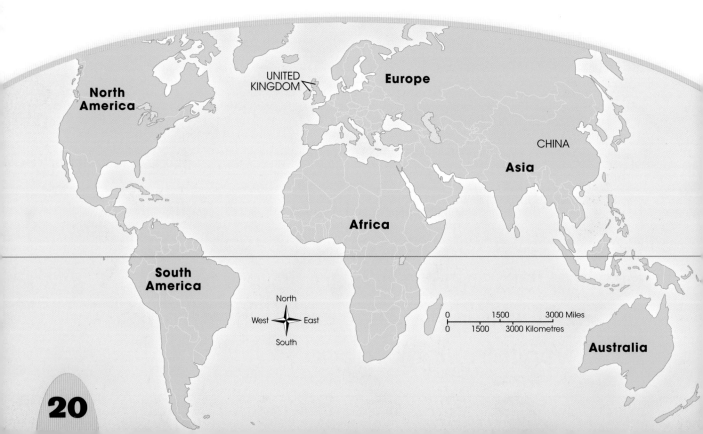

UNITED KINGDOM

Europe

North America

CHINA

Asia

Africa

South America

North

West — East

South

0   1500   3000 Miles

0   1500   3000 Kilometres

Australia

The printing company is in a big building.

The **publishing company** sends the book to the printing company over the internet. The printer gets the cover and pages with all the words and pictures in place. They are exactly the way the designer set them out.

Ink on paper

There are lots of machines doing different jobs inside the printing **factory**. Printing machines use several colours of ink to print the words and pictures of the book.

It is noisy and hot inside a printing factory. There is a strong smell of printing ink.

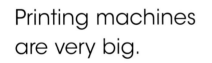

Printing machines
are very big.

Sometimes paper for printing books comes in big, flat sheets. Sometimes it comes off a massive roll in one long strip. The paper has lots of pages from the book printed on it.

Folding, cutting, and binding

When the ink is dry, machines fold the paper. They fold until the paper is the size of the book pages. Then machines cut the paper to make the page edges neat.

Look how much paper this machine cuts through at a time!

This machine makes book covers out of thick card.

The pages are sent to the bindery. This is where the book cover is bound or joined to the inside pages. Then the book is finished. The printing **factory** makes thousands of copies of the book.

Transporting the books

The finished books are packed into large cardboard boxes called cartons. The cartons are sent to the **publishing company**. They travel by ship and lorry.

Big ships carry metal containers filled with books.

The publishing company stores the books in its **warehouse**. The books go from the warehouse to libraries, schools, bookshops, and supermarkets.

Ready to read!

Customers pay the shops for the books. The shops buy the books from the **publishing company**. The publishing company uses the money to pay the printer and the team of people who made the book.

It is fun to choose a new book to read.

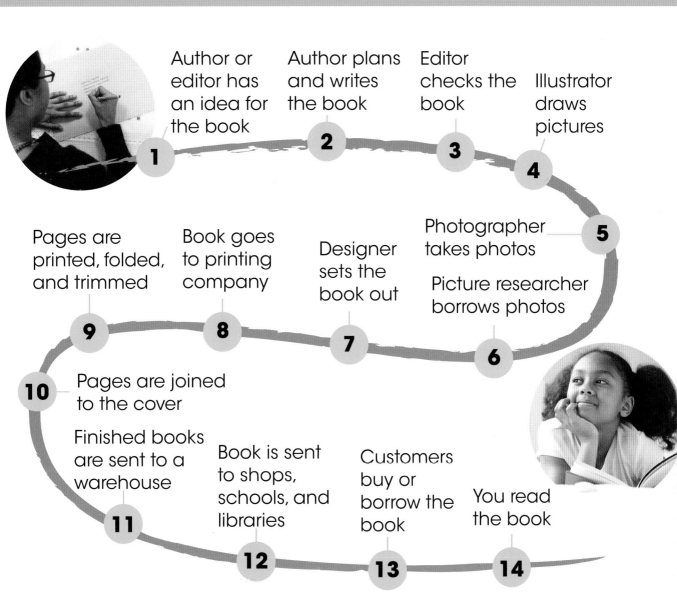

1. Author or editor has an idea for the book

2. Author plans and writes the book

3. Editor checks the book

4. Illustrator draws pictures

5. Photographer takes photos / Picture researcher borrows photos

6.

7. Designer sets the book out

8. Book goes to printing company

9. Pages are printed, folded, and trimmed

10. Pages are joined to the cover

11. Finished books are sent to a warehouse

12. Book is sent to shops, schools, and libraries

13. Customers buy or borrow the book

14. You read the book

Isn't it good to have a new book to read? Just think, your favourite **author** is probably writing a new book right now – but you'll have to wait to read it!

Glossary

author person who writes the words for a book

designer person who sets out the words and pictures for the pages of a book

editor person who works with an author, checking what he or she has written

factory building where things are made

fiction type of writing that describes imaginary people and events

font particular shape of letters used in printing

illustration picture that is drawn or painted

illustrator person who makes illustrations

imagination power of the mind to form pictures and ideas

non-fiction type of writing that describes real people and events

photographer person who takes photographs

picture researcher person who searches for pictures, especially photographs

printing company business (company) that prints the pages of books and magazines

publishing company business (company) that creates books and magazines

warehouse building where things are stored

Book quiz

1. Is this book a fiction or a non-fiction book? (see page 4)

2. Who usually has the idea for a non-fiction book? (see page 9)

3. Who writes the plan? (see page 12)

4. Who sets out the pages? (see page 18)

5. What country was this book printed in? (see page 20)

Find out more

This cartoon guide shows how a children's fiction book is made:
www.penguin.co.uk/static/misc/uk/puffin/makebook3.swf

See a printing machine at work – it's noisy!
www.youtube.com/watch?v=MR-CbgKZwhE&feature=related

Answers to quiz

1. non-fiction, 2. the editor, 3. the author, 4. the designer, 5. China

Index